THIS WALKER BOOK BELONGS TO:

_____

_____

_____

_____

To Kalera
~G.N.

To Laura and Imogen
~S.A.

First published 1997 by
Walker Books Ltd
87 Vauxhall Walk
London SE11 5HJ

This edition published 1998

10 9 8 7 6 5 4 3 2 1

Text © 1997 Grace Nichols
Illustrations © 1997 Sarah Adams

This book has been typeset
in ITC Highlander Bold.

Printed in Hong Kong

British Library Cataloguing
in Publication Data
A catalogue record for this book
is available from the British Library.

ISBN 0-7445-5498-5

ASANA
AND THE
ANIMALS
A Book of Pet Poems

Grace Nichols

illustrated by Sarah Adams

WALKER BOOKS
AND SUBSIDIARIES
LONDON • BOSTON • SYDNEY

PIT-A-PAT-A-PARROT

Pit-a-pat-a-parrot
on her parrot back
pit a little pat a little
don't forget to scratch
a little
don't forget to chat
a little
she will learn the knack
a little

If you pit-a-pat-a-parrot
if you chit-a-chat-a-parrot
while you scritch and scratch a parrot

She will chit and chat right back.

LITTLE ASANA

Little Asana sat on a sofa
eating her peas and rice.
There came a small spider
that snuggled up beside her
and Asana said, "I think you're nice."

Now little Asana is a spider-liker,
little Asana is a spider-minder,
she always keeps one close beside her.
And sometimes when she's asleep
and dreaming
her spider will take her for
a ride to the ceiling.

What Asana Wanted for Her Birthday

Please don't get me
a hamster or budgie.
Please don't get me
a goldfish or canary.

Please get me something
a little scary.
Maybe something
a wee bit hairy.

How about a tarantula?
What's wrong with a spider-pet?
If it gets sick of course
I'll take it to scare –
I mean to see
– the vet.

MY GRANDMOTHER'S CAT

Why does my grandmother always sit
with her cat in her lap?

Why does my grandmother always sit
stroking that soft, furry back?

Whenever I ask my grandmother why,
she just gives a happy sort of sigh:
"Asana, child,
  it gives me such pleasure,
    then again, it's very very good
      for my blood pressure."

GRASSHOPPER ONE

Grasshopper one
Grasshopper two
Grasshopper hopping
in the morning dew

Grasshopper three
Grasshopper four
Grasshopper stopping
by the leafy door

Grasshopper five
Grasshopper six
Grasshopper lying
like a green
matchstick

Grasshopper seven
Grasshopper eight
Grasshopper suddenly
standing up straight

Grasshopper nine
Grasshopper ten
Grasshopper,
will you be my
secret friend?

DON'T CRY CATERPILLAR

Don't cry Caterpillar
Caterpillar don't cry
You'll be a butterfly
by and by.

Caterpillar please
don't worry 'bout a thing –

"But," said the caterpillar,
"Will I still know myself
in wings?"

EVERY TIME I SEE HER

She's a slow-plodding
Chew-cudding Jersey cow
But every time I see her
I got to go – WOW!

She's calm, she's kind
She's so serene –
She's Ruler of the Pasture,
She's Queen of the Green.

Every time I see her
I just have to think –
What would be my cornflakes
without her milk?

What would be my pudding
without her cream?
She really is
A queen supreme.

She's a lovely buttery
lottery-winning cow
And every time I see her
I got to go – WOW!

DEAR HONEY-BEE

Dear Honey-bee
if I speak politely
will you still sting me?

I love the way
you dress
in your black and yellow vest

I love your
see-through wings
and everything

I love your creepy legs
(no, not creepy
just nice and shimmery)

See, Honey-bee
I'm coming ...
a little closer

But no,
I think I'd better go
back inside, Honey-bee

Goodbye.

LADYBUG

Red black-spotted Ladybug,
Can you do the jitterbug?

I've never tried the jitterbug
But when the sunlight hits my wings
You should see me do my thing,
Child, you should see me
do the Glitterbug.

HEY DIDDLE-DIDDLE

Hey diddle-diddle
the cat's on my middle
and my grandma's in the kitchen
with the spoons.

And I can't lift her off
'cause she's digging in her claws.

Grandma stop the twiddle
and take your cat from my middle.

She doesn't give a fiddle
that I want to get up
and see the moon.

WHAT ASANA SAID ABOUT THE ELEPHANTS AT THE ZOO:

Elephants are nice
because they like
to squirt themselves
with mud and dust
to protect their skin from the sun
then later on they wash it off
in splashing fun.

Can't I be a bit like the elephants, Mum?
I hate putting sunblock on.

LYING STILL IN MUDDY RIVER

Alligator
grey-green
creature
lying still
in muddy river

Pretending to be tree-trunk
but I can see your bumpety-bumps
and your long long mouth
and your half-moon eye
suddenly opening sly

Alligator
grey-green
creature
lying still
in muddy river

Not me, Asana, for your dinner.

HAVE YOU EVER SEEN?

Have you ever seen
a blue tadpole?
Have you ever seen
a spoilt-brat toad?

Have you ever seen
a walking fish?
Have you ever seen
a tricycling chick?

Have you ever seen
a rowing spider?
Have you ever seen
a dancing tiger?

Have you ever seen
a reading parrot?
Have you ever seen
a jogging ocelot?

Have you ever?

THREE LITTLE PIGS

Three little pigs starting out all new,
Three little pigs all wondering what to do,
The first built a house of straw,
Wolf ... there were two!

Two little pigs dragging their feet along,
Two little pigs singing a sad song,
The second built a house of sticks,
Wolf ... there was one!

One little pig thinking kinda quick,
One little pig going for brick,
He built a house all sturdy and thick,
Wolf ... huffed-puffed till his old jaws clicked!

Next morning the newspaper said:

CLEVER PIG GOT BAD WOLF NICKED.

AT THE BOTTOM
OF THE GARDEN

No, it isn't an old football
grown all shrunken and prickly
because it was left out so long
at the bottom of the garden.

It's only Hedgehog
who, when she thinks I'm not looking,
unballs herself to move ...
Like bristling black lightning.

If I Had a Giraffe

If I had a giraffe –
I'd climb up a ladder to her with a laugh.
I'd rest my head against her long neck,
And we'd go – riding riding riding.

We'd go anywhere under the sky,
Maybe to some faraway blue seaside,
Just to see flying fish flashing by,
And we'd go – riding riding riding.

We'd go to the land
where all fruit trees grow,
And my giraffe would stretch her neck
To get me to the highest, rosiest mango,
And we'd go – riding riding riding.

Even to the desert where the hot sands glow,
We'd go – riding riding riding –
Me and my beautiful giraffe-friend,
Whose face reminds me of a camel.

Things I Like in the Sea that Go by Swimmingly

Jellyfish
Starfish
Flying fish
Seals

Dolphins
Octopuses
Otters
Eels

Crabs
Turtles
Weevers
Manatees

Sea lions
Walruses
Shrimps
Whales

But best of all
I like Mermaids

MORE WALKER PAPERBACKS
For You to Enjoy

SING, SOPHIE!

by Dayle Ann Dodds, illustrated by Rosanne Litzinger

Little Sophie Adams loves to sing – very loudly.
The problem is none of her family want to listen!

"Bounces along with all the verve and rhythm of a country and western song…
A funny, warm-hearted read for three- to six-year-olds."
The Sunday Telegraph

0-7445-5492-6   £4.99

A CARIBBEAN DOZEN

edited by John Agard and Grace Nichols, illustrated by Cathie Felstead

Runner-up for the Mother Goose Illustration Award

"A great treat. The dozen in the title refers to the thirteen poets who are featured…
An excellent introduction to Caribbean poetry." *Morag Styles, Books for Keeps*

0-7445-5201-X   £8.99

A CUP OF STARSHINE

compiled by Jill Bennett, illustrated by Graham Percy

In this lively anthology for young children you'll find poems about subjects as diverse as
washing and springtime, playing and the moon…

"A beautifully produced and illustrated anthology." *Independent on Sunday*

0-7445-3040-7   £5.99